GIANNI VERSACE

RICHARD MARTIN

The imaginative and intelligent collections created in the 1980s and 1990s by Gianni Versace (1946-1997) have earned him a position of prominence in the history of late-twentieth century fashion. Many think of Versace primarily as flamboyant and outrageous, a designer whose sources were those of the street and popular culture. But while this is true, Versace was also as interested and knowledgeable in the history of both art and fashion as he was in Hollywood, rock, "angst" and the runway. His costumes blend past and present, high and pop culture, and the result is fashion appropriate for the nineties. He always retained a fierce individuality, unabashedly open in his penchant for sensuality in both womenswear and menswear. A regular visitor at The Metropolitan Museum of Art, he attended exhibitions at The Costume Institute with great enthusiasm and also looked at the art in other galleries avidly. He deeply admired the classicism of Madame Grès and spent hours studying her work at the Costume Institute's 1994 exhibition. In addition, Versace's last collection was partially inspired by The Metropolitan Museum of Art's 1997 exhibition "The Glory of Byzantium."

This publication and the exhibition that it accompanies commemorate Versace's unique achievement, placing him for the first time in the realm of the museum and of history. Gone are the super-models, the glitz of the media, and the spectacle of the runways, but the splendor remains in Versace's creations, even when seen as they are in the pages of this book, stripped of their previous accoutrements and elegantly displayed on museum mannequins.

Richard Martin, Curator in Charge, The Costume Institute, The Metropolitan Museum of Art, has written a conceptual and analytical text that both places Versace's work in historical context and provides new insights into the major inspirations and themes of the designer. In the Introduction, he discusses Versace's relationship with earlier designers' work, and he also clarifies Versace's metamorphosis of the prostitute into a positive, even exuberant expression of glamor and of independence from middle-of-the-road values. The body of the book is divided into seven conceptual sections, each beginning with a text summarizing the topic and each also including a brief discussion of individual costumes, all of

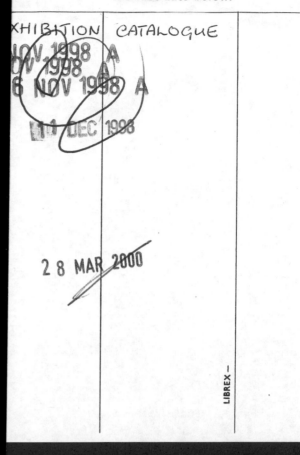

Gianni Versace

GIANNI VERSACE

RICHARD MARTIN

PHOTOGRAPHS BY KARIN L. WILLIS

THE METROPOLITAN MUSEUM OF ART, NEW YORK
DISTRIBUTED BY HARRY N. ABRAMS, INC., NEW YORK

This volume has been published in conjunction with the exhibition "Gianni Versace," held at The Metropolitan Museum of Art from December 11, 1997, through March 22, 1998.

The exhibition is made possible by CONDÉ NAST and The David H. Koch Charitable Foundation.

Additional support has been provided by Fairchild Publications and VH1.

Published by The Metropolitan Museum of Art, New York

John P. O'Neill, Editor in Chief
Barbara Cavaliere, Editor
Design by Matsumoto Incorporated, New York
Gwen Roginsky and Rich Bonk, Production

Copyright © The Metropolitan Museum of Art, New York

Library of Congress Cataloging-in-Publication Data

Martin, Richard
    Gianni Versace / Richard Martin.
            p. cm.
    Catalog accompanying an exhibition at The Metropolitan Museum of Art, Dec. 11, 1997, to Mar. 22, 1998.
        Includes bibliographical references.
        ISBN 0–87099–842–0.—
        ISBN 0–87099–843–9 (pbk.).—
        ISBN 0–8109–6521–6 (Abrams)
        1. Versace, Gianni—Exhibitions. 2. Costume design—Italy—History—20th century—Exhibitions. 3. Fashion designers—Italy—Exhibitions. I. Versace, Gianni. II. Metropolitan Museum of Art (New York, N.Y.) III. Title.
TT502.M3713   1997
746.9'2'092—dc21   97–32249
                                    CIP

The photography in this volume is by Karin L. Willis, The Photograph Studio, The Metropolitan Museum of Art.

All the costumes in this volume are in the collection of The Costume Institute, The Metropolitan Museum of Art, or Courtesy Gianni Versace Archives.

Color separations by Professional Graphics, Rockford, Illinois
Printed on Consort Royal Silk 150 gsm
Printed by Julio Soto Impresor, S.A., Madrid
Bound by Encuadernación Ramos, S.A., Madrid
Printing and binding coordinated by Ediciones El Viso, S.A., Madrid

Cover: Detail of page 18

Frontispiece: Detail of page 44

Contents

Condé Nast and VOGUE magazine are privileged to honor and celebrate the late designer Gianni Versace's remarkable legacy to the world of fashion by co-sponsoring The Costume Institute's 1997 exhibition "Gianni Versace" at The Metropolitan Museum of Art.

The exhibition, which had always been a dream of Gianni's, a longtime supporter of The Costume Institute himself, traces his lifetime of work and his extraordinary career. "Gianni Versace" reflects the designer's major themes, monuments, and inspirations from both art and history. Our sponsorship of "Gianni Versace" is a bittersweet tribute to a man whose commitment and contributions to the art of fashion will be deeply missed.

FOREWORD

As a museum director, I occasionally long to celebrate all of those ardent and frequent visitors who love The Metropolitan Museum of Art and learn endlessly from its collections and exhibitions. In this instance, I have the rare pleasure of commending one such visitor, Gianni Versace (1946–1997). Versace was an avid fan of the Museum, even using in his last couture collection the Byzantine crosses that he remembered seeing in "The Glory of Byzantium" exhibition a few months before. Also, Versace gave generously to The Costume Institute, always offering to the collection the pieces requested by The Costume Institute's curator. He was a generous patron to the 1995–96 exhibition "Haute Couture."

The exhibition "Gianni Versace" is, of course, not about his love of The Metropolitan Museum of Art but about the Museum's admiration for Versace. As the exhibition demonstrates, Versace earned, despite his early and tragic death, a place in fashion history. He created design at every level and in a variety of media, expanding in later years into home furnishings and tableware. But his essential craft was always the clothing.

In this exhibition and book we see the Versace garment no longer on the luminous runways, on supermodels and superstars, or with the benefit of lavish "image" campaigns and advertising icons. As always, The Costume Institute serves as the place where fashion is rendered inanimate yet with no loss of splendor or magic for the purpose of study. The truth is that Versace does not need the aura and charisma that he prized and used to benefit the clothing. Subjected to the analytical examination of our exhibition, dresses in plastic, boisterous appropriations from contemporary art and art history, and tour-de-force dresses with safety-pin bridges across skin resonate not with spectacle alone but with introspection and serious intelligence. Years ago, Richard Martin, Curator of The Costume Institute, wrote that "Versace's clothing is far less diva and dominatrix than it might seem." That assessment is borne out in an exhibition rich with historical influences from Poiret, Grès, and Vionnet as well as versatile in suits, evening dresses, and daywear.

In September, The Metropolitan Museum of Art was the site of Gianni Versace's American memorial, a very private and moving ceremony. There, we said farewell. In this exhibition, we acclaim and applaud a lifetime of bold artistic exploration worthy of fashion history. Indeed, this exhibition should also be viewed as a commitment on the part of The Costume Institute to display more frequently in the future contemporary fashion design in its exhibition program.

The Museum gratefully acknowledges substantial support from Condé Nast and The David H. Koch Charitable Foundation. Additional assistance was received from Fairchild Publications Inc. and VH1, and we extend our most appreciative thanks for their generosity.

Philippe de Montebello
Director
The Metropolitan Museum of Art

Fashion, the art that affords inclusion, delineates individuals, and constitutes protocol, has changed fundamentally in our time. Strategies of beauty in the 1980s transformed fashion in the most important way since its transfiguration from a class system to a mass consumption energy in the late 1960s. Gianni Versace reorganized the etiquette of apparel. He did not aspire to decorum. Rather, he accorded fashion with desire, substituting the lust of fashion and body concupiscence for the cause of correct behavior and social calibration.

In wanting to bestow upon Versace his grand place in fashion history, one cannot forget that modern fashion has not always been prim or sedate. Those who contrived to situate it back into place as a criterion for enforcing systems of pseudo-aristocracies of the 1970s and 1980s were the ones with short fashion memories. Versace's *épater la bourgeoisie* stance commands the longer history of modern fashion: it is not polite but aggressive. Father Abraham to the fashion genealogy, Charles Frederick Worth did not adhere to class distinctions. The rise of the couture accompanied the new monies and flailing monarchies of the middle years of the nineteenth century. Worth was dressing the imperial courts, the "best" ladies, and the very "best" courtesans and stage performers. The client list that established the modern art of fashion was as cross-cultural as Edouard Manet's contemporaneous vision. A century earlier, fashion had been associated with moral vituperation, denounced when convenient as an instrument of economic tyranny. Worth pulled fashion away from its elitist constituencies and moral function.

Versace posed and provoked the basic issues of fashion's role. Versace tantalized us with vulgarity. In this, he adapted a strategy from the fine arts in the twentieth century, including elements of the banal and coarse in his sensibility. The collage, smarmy joke, offensive imagery, and ready-made object pertinent in the juggernaut of modern art are evidence of an attempt to be vulgar. Versace employed a similar strategy, perhaps to determine an audience like that of contemporary art with its feint to the liberal left designed to evade at each step the possibility of becoming a bourgeois commodity.

Modern art found one great ideal in the prostitute. As Toulouse-Lautrec discovered the aesthetic probity of the demimonde and the ideal model in the streetwalker during the 1880s and 1890s, so too Versace located the prostitute as the last unexamined figure in fashion's twenty-year sociology of the street. Yves Saint Laurent had plucked trenchant elements of fashion from the denizens of the street, day and night, rendering glamorous the effects of sailors, drag kings, and men in black. Later, in the 1970s and 1980s, Rei Kawakubo sagaciously surveyed the street for the vitality in the swaggering and provisional drape of the displaced and the punk, much in the manner of Manet's epic scanning in the 1860s. By the 1980s, Jean Paul Gaultier was collecting from the street for his zany anthropology of a complex, pluralistic modern life.

But with all of this scavenging of the street for transfiguration into style, one creature of every street metaphor remained untouched. Versace found her as a boy on the streets of Reggio Calabria and never forgot her confident style. He saw her in the great films of Federico Fellini, Luchino Visconti, and others who defined the Italian postwar cinema as an international success. He saw her in the new license of sex worker, gender-proud and gender-heroic, in the sexually liberated world of the 1970s and 1980s. She is Mary Magdalen and Vivian Ward *Pretty Woman* (1990), the prostitute not only with a heart of gold but with a gold mine of design ideas as well. No one had taken the prostitute into fashion as Versace did. In a feat worthy of literature, Versace seized the streetwalker's bravado and conspicuous wardrobe, along with her blatant, brandished sexuality, and introduced them into high fashion.

But Versace did not, like some of his followers, simply convey the prostitute to the salon and runway. He did what fashion can do when it finds inspiration on the street. He represented her as glamor, accepting the extreme flirtatiousness of short skirts, the seduction of shiny cloth and cognate materials, and understanding the motive of sex, but rendering each hyperbolic and expressive, not merely a portrayal of what had existed in the wardrobe of the street. Versace gave as much to the prostitute as he took from her style. He supplied her with a new suppleness that made the body-clinging drapery work in the manner of early Madame Grès. He worked the transparency of lace with the shine of metal mesh as if to both dazzle and seduce the prostitute's client in one fell swoop. He accommodated her lack of expertise and her excess in pattern mixing with design juxtapositions that are extravagant but not clashing. He made her in rich silk and long gown with a train that is a cross between Cinderella and Delilah.

Prostitute style was always present on the Versace runway. Soon after she was concocted in the 1980s, she was melded into runway glamor by the thin nonchalance of high-fashion models and the spectacle of the mediagenic fashion show. By the beginning of the 1990s, she had almost lost her original identity, as if she had immediately been accepted in late-twentieth-century society as a tycoon's ravishing second wife, regardless of background. But art museums are, of course, filled with portraits of prostitutes and parvenues, their posings always most interesting because of their aspirations. We could hardly imagine the history of modern art without those flagrantly tawdry women who came to define the progressive and transgressive limning of the modern.

In making his deliberate choice to exalt the streetwalker, Versace risked the opprobrium of the bourgeoisie. As a designer and as a human being, Versace never sought the middle road or the middle class. Rather, he forged a unity between the independent of spirit and will, the rich, the young, and the intrepid. Without explicitly rejecting the bourgeoisie, he never affiliated his fashion with conventional sensibility and never was grounded in the proprieties that middle-class values implicate. In fact, it is the middle class alone that still withholds its approval from Versace, often distancing itself from his purported vulgarity and his unabashed embrace of consumption. When one considers that fashion designers of the past who were enthusiastically welcomed by the bourgeoisie, such as Christian Dior and Cristobal Balenciaga, posed uncouth décolletage or peasant inspirations for high fashion, we understand the special case of Versace. Like Chanel, he ensnared more than fashion. He was defining the character of the modern woman, reassigning power, and infusing lifestyle issues into the fabric of clothing. His valorization of the prostitute was an exquisite choice, recognizing the independence and strength of the streetwalker not as an enslaved sex worker but as an autonomous, self-defining figure of awesome visual authority among the ambiguous and compromised figures of modern visual culture.

For even beyond playing Pygmalion to the prostitute, Versace was, like Chanel some fifty years before, enlisting sex into fashion. It is said that Chanel designed a skirt with a bit of concavity at center front not merely for suppleness in appearance but also to remind the viewer of the woman's body. She was not the analytical cubist striving for abstract cones and cylinders; she was the sensuous feminist, acknowledging an inner truth to the body underlying the clothing. Likewise, Versace's sensuous drapery of the 1980s and 1990s revels in the body within; it falls onto the body not as a scrim but as three-dimensional teasing veils. For example, a leather and lace dress with net midriff inevitably becomes a moiré pattern contingent on the pressure and release of the body underneath. Yet, even again like Chanel, Versace lived to see his initially deemed outrageous work grow to be accepted. *New York Times* fashion writer Amy Spindler (August 5, 1997) wrote, after Versace's death: "What was so jarring about much of his work in the 1980s was that he used references that at the time were unacceptable in designer fashion: leather, denim, brash prints, bondage, metal mesh, and even sexiness that, for its time, was considered 'happy hooker' lewd. Time made those references part of the standard fashion vocabulary."

Recognizing Versace as the first post-Freudian designer is honoring the truth and utter lack of shame or guilt in him. The moral, religious, or decorous reticence and remorse of other fashion about sex is lacking in Versace. He accepted sex not merely as a fact of life but as a celebration of life. The long tradition of fashion's coy expression of sexuality, alluding as by metaphor to sex, is ultimately grounded in the conventions of refinement. By those conventions, Versace is raw and impudent. Yet it would be hard to imagine the cultural construction by which in the 1980s and 1990s refinement denies sexuality. Further, Versace's candor and the primacy he gave to sexuality apply to men as well as women. His menswear designs suggest the same forthright eroticism that he exercised in womenswear. He would not tolerate repressed sexuality for either men or women.

Central to Versace's work is his acuity in understanding fashion as an art of the media. Not only did he thrust fashion into the gobbling jaws of the media of the contemporary spectacle in runway shows and alliances with rock music, dance, and performance, he also grasped and was empathetic to the charisma of media performers. While other fashion designers have also understood the media's attraction for fashion, Versace was a virtuoso performer in this regard. The clothes address this role for they—at least, the most familiar garments—are seldom made for the polite drawing-room discourse or even the private ballroom candlelight of most fashion design. Rather, they radiate under the lights of the camera, of the runway, and of video's revealing eye. Versace designed for the visually voracious, media-saturated generations that have come of age only in the last quarter of the twentieth century. No other time could have convened fashion of plastic, intended for spectacular effect, and grand dresses designed for an opulence not only in the details but also in the effect and charismatic afterlife of the image. Versace knew that fashion could participate in the great *Gesamtkunstwerk* of the end of the millennium that had recruited equal parts of rock, special effects, the cult of personality, and unadulterated eroticism. Versace put fashion into that farrago not as an ancillary measure but at parity with all the other arts of media dynamic. Media discernment may, in some ways, displace the social judgment implicit in most fashion. In social terms, plastic is an inappropriate material for dress. In media terms, plastic provides the excitements of sheen and muted transparency. Hence, Versace played with plastic skins combined with silk linings. Leather, still bold in the social setting, stimulates media tumult and suggests power. Versace reads at least as forcefully from the distance of media as from the traditionally closer proximity of social relationships. It is as if the designer had an instinctive media sense for the perception of fashion, the art that he practiced at hand in draping but that he also perceived from afar in synergy with media.

In the deliberate choice in this book to represent Versace's work on mannequins rather than on the famous super-models in fashion photography, we have pursued fashion as a still life. The evidence provided by these images is that Versace offers impact and excitement even when detached from the seeming codependency of media energy. To bring Versace to the museological preserve denies nothing of the inherent animation of his work. Deprived of the stars, his landmarks are still indispensable documents of style in our time. Divested of the designer's undeniable personal charisma, the clothing remains important and elegant.

If media augmented fashion's expectation of spectatorship from a social distance, it has been not only fashion's observer but also its genesis. As early as the 1980s, Versace was creating to the scale of film. His several affiliations with dance and opera certify that he could demand that clothing be read on proscenium, but he also knew that clothing ideas came not only from the garment but from film and media as well. His admiration for Grès and Vionnet always had a touch of Hollywood and Jean Harlow added, thus reinvesting his clothes with movie-star sensuality. He envisioned fashion as if it were appearing in a movie or video, in the extreme and the representational, not merely in the ideal paradigm of apparel. The drapery in his metallic slave-girl dresses is not Greek or Roman, though Versace did understand and enlarge upon the principle of classical wet-drapery. Versace was also versed in gladiator films: his historicism is thorough and knowing, but by the end of the twentieth century, historicism necessarily includes the media's dilations of "real" history into hyperbolic and imagined history. Similarly, Versace's inspirations from the eighteenth century glow as if for the candlelight of court chambers and ballrooms while commanding as well the spotlight of the modern spectacle.

On seeing his work in a museum exhibition or in this book, it becomes clear that Gianni Versace is not merely a figure of sentiment or cultural inquiry, or subject-object of the media spectacle. Under the dissecting light of a museum's examination, Versace achieves another and equally positive effect. The encyclopedic knowledge, the virtuoso performance of techniques, the sensibility to experiment, and the equilibrium between history and contemporaneity are perhaps seen even more clearly here. Thus, his landmarks must hold their own without the presence of the celebrities or circumstances that inaugurated them or that burnished them in memory. The inspirations from art are not to be museum equivalents, but they must now represent something more than runway souvenirs that reference art. Experiments in materials and in the transubstantiation of reality into fantasy and opera-scale theatricality must be plausible as avant-gardism or as performance documents. The fashion designer who so embodied the vitality of recent years continues to transmit that same quality on mannequins and in a museum setting. Cynics say of contemporary fashion, especially of Versace: take away the rock and roll, the advertising budgets, and the super-models, and what have you got? They expect the answer to be: nothing. For Versace, the answer is: incredible fashion that answers still to the indomitable spirit of century's finale.

Evening gown (side detail),
spring–summer 1994
Black silk with silver and gold-tone
metal safety-pin ornaments
Courtesy Gianni Versace Archives

Chanel's little black dress was
revolutionary as social statement about
the economic upheaval of the 1920s, but
it has long since lost its socio-economic
sting. Like all that becomes popular, it
has been absorbed into cultural
acceptance with null radicalism. Versace
opened up the little black dress to a
fresher revolution, anathema to the
middle class in the 1990s. After more
than sixty years, the little black dress is
flagrantly voluptuous.

Every designer creates landmark pieces, charting the course of his or her
design evolution. Because of the public designer that Gianni Versace was
in the 1980s and 1990s, his landmarks were imposed, even more than
exposed, on the common memory. Almost anyone can recall with
vividness the first impressions of the benchmark works that were truly
seen around the world. Versace's ethos of the spectacular and his feeling
for an eye-scorching cultural and aesthetic avant-gardism, always
venturing into the most hyperbolic form of any style, made it seem that his
work would defy any retrospective. Yet, in a certain sense, the landmarks
do stand as a brief retrospective of the designer's work.

Today, we perceive Versace landmarks without the corollary media
sensationalism and even, to some degree, without their being inhabited by
the most beautiful and the most famous. They stand alone as design
objects. Richard Avedon, Irving Penn, Bruce Weber, and other leading
photographers have so successfully and compellingly acquainted us with
Versace that the existing photographic icons have deliberately not been
employed here in order to enforce new and sustained examination.

Amy Spindler of the *New York Times*, in a retrospective article
"Versace's Errors Showed Him a Way" (August 5, 1997), saw the Versace
method as one of experiment, design labor, refinement, and ultimate
success. Spindler argued that no idea, once tried, was ever wholly
abandoned and that, in the manner of any laboratory for experiment, one
could observe favored ideas improving in form over time. Versace's

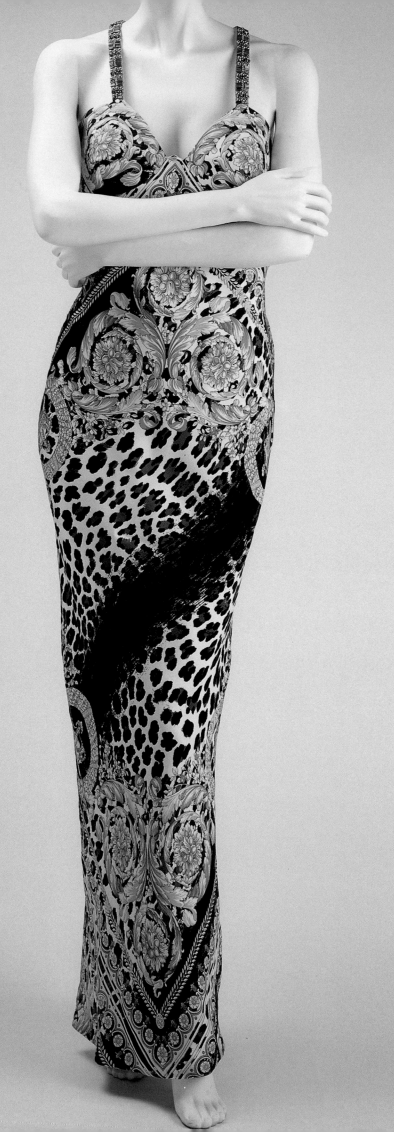

Evening gown, ca. 1992
Brown, white, and gold leopard-printed
and baroque-pattern-printed silk
microfaille with beaded shoulder straps
Courtesy Gianni Versace Archives

To dress in little more than a scarf is not
merely akin to Salome's dance; it is also
in tune with the simplifying ambition of
much modern fashion. A fancy, even
flashy, scarf is diagonally disposed to
become the basis of this dress, already
possessing the gold overlay and border,
animal print, and dynamic required to
make a dress as Versace made dresses, by
the age-old process of draping.

landmarks are of such complexity, for they are not necessarily the only
versions of the ideas in question, but rather they are what seem to be some
of the most important and compelling forms of the continuing experiment.
Thus, a selection of Versace's landmarks demonstrates the designer's
eclectic but tenacious interests, often expressed in series and occasionally
in single pieces. But the singles are the exception, for Versace never
believed in and seldom accepted "well enough." His opulent prints are
bold enough to encompass gilded neoclassicism and wild-animal prints,
baroque fetes and the exaggerated resort style of South Beach, rich
classical imagery and the patterns of Ravenna mosaics. The puncturings
and suturings of Versace's sui generis high punk, confecting a high art
where the style and impulse had never reached above class and adolescent
rebellions, are a complete transfiguration of their source materials. The
punk impulse to accumulate and tether was an additive strategy. Versace
took the element of suturings and fastenings to his eternal impetus to let
the body break through the barrier of clothing. His extravagant
appropriations from popular culture are characteristic of many of
Versace's most innovative work. Though the idea pre-existed in some way,
he manipulated the reasoning and the fulfillment of the form, ending with
a landmark that is genuinely Versace. It is not surprising that the 1996 art-
fashion conjunction in Florence juxtaposed Roy Lichtenstein and Versace.
Both artists were respectful of the past but insistent on the right to
reinterpret pre-existing images in their work, often bringing the dull and

uninflected art of the commonplace into an extreme, hyperbolic form.

Of course, to determine which punk-inspired garment is the landmark, given the designer's insistence on perfecting an idea on his own terms, is a difficult task. Among the great sari dresses, there must be some choice, but the designer played with the sari as a composer plays with sonata form. Here, the slashing and violation of the age-old form carry a political implication, and Versace pointedly confronted the eternity of the sari with the ephemerality of punk. With the criticality worthy of a philosopher holding two principles in opposition and determining some adjudication between the two but an appreciation of both, Versace created a synthesis of a 1970s London and an India of the Raj or of even more primal times.

But there is also an irrefutable memory to Versace's ultimate draping with pin-bridged openings. The Elizabeth Hurley dress (1994) emerges from the sari development, but it is of another, quite remarkable synapse in the designer's keen mind. The color and drape of the sari are eschewed in favor of the little black dress. Versace opened up the side from bust to waist and again at the upper leg. Versace's dress is as startling in design conception as it was arresting when seen on Hurley. The little black dress is almost as much a tradition, at least for the twentieth century, as is the sari and likewise connotes convention and implacable design. Versace attacked the little black dress savagely, letting go of Chanel's coy sensuality through suppleness and elasticity and unleashing a body-exposing,

Day ensemble, fall–winter 1991–92
Black silk twill printed with gold baroque motifs
Courtesy Gianni Versace Archives

The gold classicism and gold baroque that became signatures for Versace recur again and again. Symbols of the comfort and opulence that Versace wanted to project, they migrate from scarves and accessories into the clothing and back again. In the 1990s, they also inhabit Versace interiors and tableware designs. This day ensemble is able to convey the essence of the designer simply by the talismanic quality of its baroque elements.

Evening ensemble, spring–summer 1996
Zebra-printed synthetic stretch mesh,
yellow-and-black leopard-printed silk
Courtesy Gianni Versace Archives

Amazing and sensuous combinations are
characteristic of Versace. Polite matching
was a trifle to Versace. He preferred the
surprise, even the initial dissonance, of
unexpected and frenetic combinations.
His disposition to pose the controversial
rather than the polite and conventional is
at the heart of every design decision, even
including the uproarious pattern mix.

process-displaying working method. Thus, it is ironic to think of a Versace
creation as a landmark, inasmuch as his work was so often about
demolishing landmarks in contemporary fashion.

Similarly, Versace's remarkable corset and lingerie dresses are not
merely like those of the many contemporary designers who were still, in
the 1980s and 1990s, stimulated by antique lingerie redesigned at its own
scale to a single-layer dressing. Versace extended the corset to function
as an evening dress, establishing a newly sinuous line from the bust to
the toes.

Versace's landmarks are not definitive. Rather, they are only
moments from a rich, varied scrapbook of remembrances that can take any
spectator into the realm of memory and yield even more through their
knowledge of design history.

Evening dress, spring–summer 1994
Yellow-and-orange crimped synthetic
jersey
Gift of Gianni Versace, 1996
(1996.202.3)

Crimped jersey sets in the wrinkles that
imply a first order of disarray. Versace
reified the process by using grandiose
punk safety-pins as if they are a part of
the draping process. Thus, he set the
dress out as if it were the most
rudimentary process of the draping
imagination, using studio discards for
material. Elsewhere, the safety-pins offer
their curious dialogue between the faux-
elegant and the practical, but here their
role is to render the gist of draping on
the mannequin.

**Evening gown and shorts ensemble,
spring–summer 1994**
Purple, orange, and yellow crimped
synthetic jersey
Gift of Gianni Versace, 1996
(1996.202.1 a–c)

Versace confronted two histories, one
monumental and one quite recent. The
sari represents the grand tradition of
wrapping in Indian dress. It is vitiated by
the ruptures and their closure with the
gargantuan safety pins that allude to
Versace's caricatural reference to punk,
itself a recent and ephemeral British
style. Further, there is another classic
confrontation: that the disestablishment
character of punk assails the eternity of
the sari as a way of dressing. While
Versace did not function explicitly as a
historian, he performed a critical task by
means of the elements he put together
and reconciled, at least for the purpose
of the dress itself.

Evening gown, spring–summer 1994
Black silk with silver and gold-tone
metal safety-pin ornaments
Courtesy Gianni Versace Archives

Perhaps forever to be known as the
Elizabeth Hurley dress, as it was first
worn by her in 1994, this dress is the
definitive resolution of Versace's use of
punk safety pins. That the British model
took the design home in a sense to
England is paradoxical, for what is
manifestly high style in this instance has
lowly British roots. But what had been a
sari or other fashion classic is now
resolutely the little black dress, its
simplicity providing the perfect foil for
the intensity of Versace's safety-pin detail
with the body's presence showing
through from beneath. Just as Gabrielle
Chanel rendered her little black dresses
as the tabula rasa on which a whole
panoply of costume jewelry and
idiosyncratic personal style could take
place, Versace rendered the little black
dress more revealing and more
voluptuous than ever.

Evening dress, fall–winter 1991–92
Quilted black silk crêpe, chiffon, and
reembroidered lace
Gift of Gianni Versace, 1993 (1993.52.5)

With a nod to the Balenciaga baby doll
of the 1950s, Versace extended the lace
of lingerie to make a skirt for the
modified form of a back-laced corset.
Imparting utmost elegance to what is a
combination of historical styles, Versace
reinforced a conceptual premise with the
employment of a multitude of beautiful
details. He pointedly never held history
up to ridicule. Rather, he celebrated
traditional technical virtuosity and
historical styles within the embrace of his
own time.

Studded ensemble, fall–winter 1991–92
Black leather and silk crepe with silver
and gold-tone metal studs
Courtesy Gianni Versace Archives

Studding, a practical reinforcement,
became design for Versace. A fret along
the hem and patterns on sleeves and
front represent Versace's talent for
turning the rugged sportswear motif into
a decorative one, treating the studding as
if it were a form of printing. The
triumph of the ensemble—and a surprise
in fashion history—is that Versace made

new ornamentation from the obdurate
and practical device of the studs. A
corresponding detail only confirms that
there is a visual delight found where we
expected only physical reinforcement. If
the effect is more Greek than Byzantine,
the idea owes something to the cognate
Byzantine pieces in the same collection,
in which mosaic tesserae are implicated
into metal on fabric and leather. Here,
classicism and ornament are discovered
in the same principle of small metal
details being read as design.

Day dress, ca. 1984
Polychrome-striped silk
Gift of Marilyn Linzer, 1996
(1996.496.1)

Big shoulders, which Versace
remembered fondly as one of his
hallmarks in the late 1970s and early
1980s, conform to the 1940s look that
Versace admired early in his career.
Movies, both Italian and American in
this case, contributed to this imagery
made especially graphic by stripes and
the relaxed disposition radiating from a
flaccid center front. Merging the easy
nonchalance of the soft silk with the
regimentation of stripes, Versace enjoyed
the sportswear graphic, while yielding to
the draping of the 1930s and 1940s.

Day dress ensemble, spring–summer 1980
Navy-and-white striped sheer silk chiffon, with red cotton-blend knit, blue leather and coral plastic accessories
Gift of Gianni Versace, 1980
(1980.399.1 a–e)

The early work of Versace includes expert sportswear, combining disparate materials with the virtuoso hand of the American sportswear pioneers. Chiffon, plastic, and leather are all used in an ensemble that bespeaks utility and semaphore-like clarity. Considering such work in the development of Versace's oeuvre, one realizes the latent sexuality in his sheer panels of cloth, bare interstices, and joyous materials.

Day pant ensemble, spring–summer 1980
Navy-and-white striped sheer chiffon
and red cotton knit
Gift of Gianni Versace, 1980
(1980.399.2 a–f)

The nautical forthrightness of this sports ensemble demonstrates Versace's early and outstanding ability to make the ordinary luxurious. Capacious pants, sheer chiffon, and soft wrapping give the outfit the utmost elegance along with comfort. Here, what comes close to a cliché of summer dressing is saved by its reliance on the unpretentious mix of ordinary and exceptional elements.

Evening gown, fall–winter 1987–88
Black metallic mesh with rhinestone and
reembroidered cotton lace trim
Gift of Gianni Versace, 1993 (1993.52.6)

The way this dress clings across the
poitrine and glistens with mesh brilliance
might suggest Versace's icon of the
prostitute, but the fineness of the lace
trim and retardataire train suggests the
delicacy of Boué Soeurs or Callot Soeurs
in the style of a court-presentation dress.
Once again, Versace attributed so much
cognition and so much fashion history to
the visionary prostitute that she became
the paradox of the woman of the night,
paragon of history. Nonetheless,
Versace's keen fondness could not be
excused by some critics, who could
hardly see the historicism for the sense
that this might be a less than proper
dress. Versace would never exculpate nor
be disdainful of the prostitute: it is her
presence as ideal that prevented Versace
from ever being bourgeois.

Sleeveless dress
Top-stitched lavender silk
Courtesy Gianni Versace Archives

The attentuated effect of lingerie is
achieved by extending what seem to be
the functional lines of the lingerie into
the long verticals of this dress. With
the extension of these lines, the dress
becomes both a column and an item
of lingerie, beginning to rationalize its
length and taking advantage of the
shaping lines found in lingerie
construction, here rendered
large and long.

Evening gown, fall–winter 1991–92
White silk crêpe and ribbed silk with
rhinestone grommets and shoulder straps
Gift of Gianni Versace, 1993 (1993.52.3)

Amidst the flurry of 1990s fashion
stimulated by newly supple and
externalized corsetry, Versace boldly
extended the line of the corset into a
gown. In so doing, he did not resort to
the body exaggerations of supported
bust or narrowed waist of other
practitioners of the 1990s corset. Instead,
he allowed the line to be sinuously
modern. In a sense, Versace was doing
what many other designers were doing at
the same time, but he was steadfast to
his ideal of the sensuous, body-revealing
dress, not employing the caricatural body
of many who explored body shaping.

Evening gown (detail), spring–summer 1991
Partially beaded silk twill printed with
polychrome images
Gift of Gianni Versace, 1993 (1993.52.4)

Versace's passion for Andy Warhol was
fueled, as the designer reported, by one
of his first trips to New York and his
association of Warhol with media
awareness, a lively art scene, appreciation
of art and design, and the synthesis of art
and living that Warhol practiced and that
was epitomized by the Factory. Versace, the
great observer and trawler after cultural
details, saw Warhol as a soul mate. It is no
accident that the Warhol dresses appear in
the same collection as the *Vogue* dresses. In
each case, the designer assumed media and
visual culture. The pairing of James Dean
and Marilyn Monroe is like the Pop Art
Medusa already an icon for Versace. In
1991, Versace selected classic Warhol
images that originated in the 1960s

Art excited Gianni Versace. He responded as connoisseur, enthusiast,
collector, and designer. From among all those roles, it was always Versace
the designer who was most stimulated by art. He seized with alacrity any
opportunity to work with an artist.

While Versace's historical episodes depend upon a respect for art
history, the specific interest and joy in Versace's collecting and in his
absorption of art into the design process is the modern tradition, from
Gustav Klimt, Robert Delaunay, and Alexander Calder earlier in the
century to Andy Warhol and Jim Dine later. When challenged by one of
the artists he had championed and collected and whose motifs he had used
in his work, Versace replied that art was for everyone, for sharing, and for
the lengthening of pleasure. Versace was such an idealist about art. Even if
the position is difficult for an artist to understand, as he or she watches
work achieve profits for others, Versace's largesse about art is evident in
his work and life. His keen sense of synaesthesia encouraged collaboration
with ballet and opera; his profound gratitude to the image-makers led him
to support photographic exhibitions and publications.

His multiple roles regarding art did create confusion for some. The
generous collector and benefactor could hardly seem to be the same man
who could seize upon an artist's ideas and render them into cloth with
acknowledgment, but without copyright and licensing transactions. As
Versace elsewhere seized the oxygen and aura—*l'air du temps*—of
contemporary culture for his energy and design, so too he felt that the

Evening dress, fall–winter 1984–85
Gray, yellow, and silver metal mesh
Courtesy Gianni Versace Archives

As the metal mesh became a virtuoso material for Versace, he found its inherent properties. He considered in this case, first, the rectangle, and created a silhouette attentive to the straight line and right angle. But inevitably, this reference is to the field of painting, and its decoration is now in the manner of Gustav Klimt and other decorative painters. Acceding to flatness and the rectangle, Versace did what every good modernist of art critic Clement Greenberg's orientation does and realized the full potential of flat surface.

Promethean fire of art was merely another ember for his torchy fashion. While Versace loved art and was always an avid museum goer, he did not observe the distinction that many place between popular culture and the high culture of art. In being so willing to take on art, he was not intimidated by museum solemnity nor even art's stern auteur sovereignty; it was all merely another captivating image for Versace. Characteristic is Versace's habit of visiting The Metropolitan Museum of Art in recent years, most often starting with The Costume Institute but proceeding to other galleries as well. The seamless flow of a visit to the multifarious Metropolitan Museum offers all the arts equally for the designer's consideration, so that one art is not perceived sacrosanct and another merely métier.

For each Versace example inspired by art, there is not only the paradigm but also the designer's impulse and his remodeling of it into a living art. Thus, the fragile, air-driven constellation of a Calder mobile is translated into a soft, floating, tissue-like dress that allows us to feel a gentle motion akin to that of a mobile. As Amy Spindler (*New York Times*, January 21, 1997) described: "Mr. Versace made walking mobiles of his models, in airy translucent dresses painted with Calder forms and wires." It is precisely the animation that Spindler described that is the designer's necessary objective in using art authentically: to render it in conjunction with the living model and to allow it to live in a new way. Now the Calder mobile is not merely suspended from the ceiling but dances on a strapless gown of gossamer tissue. Likewise, the rich faceting of Delaunay as practiced by Versace mediates Robert Delaunay's ideas and the brilliant textile inventions of his fellow artist Sonia Delaunay. There is no passivity in Versace's use of these artists; there is instead a capturing of the essence and a desire to see an art translated into apparel made for spectacle.

Perhaps Versace's most famous art equivalence is with Andy Warhol. Cavalier and commercial creatives both, they are less a design odd-couple than one might imagine. Instigators and voyeurs, they both were charmed by and became agents for the popular culture. In the same manner in which it is impossible for the contemporary conceptual artist to come of age without a Duchampianism, sometimes derivative, a contemporary artist of media proclivity cannot come of age without a Warholianism, most likely derivative, and Warhol served Versace both as affinity and explanation. His Pop Art dresses testify to Versace's place in the world. They bear their own sensationalism a quarter of a century after Warhol's brazen gestures. Even beyond their specific renderings—conflating James Dean and Marilyn Monroe, trumping Warhol to the later cultural exaggeration and excess, even beyond that of the 1960s—the Warhol apparel comprises Versace's declaration that fashion is to art what art was once to the popular culture—sordid scavenger and beautiful correspondent, both at once.

Day dress, spring–summer 1983
Black linen
Gift of Carol R. Reiss, 1994
(1994.472.3 a,b)

For Versace, a linen dress is as simple as
a Barnett Newman painting, which is to
say that it is calculated and contemplated
to every measurement and variation.
Like Claire McCardell, Bonnie Cashin,
and other pioneers in American
sportswear, Versace used the precise
measure of apron- and kimono-like folds
in determining unpretentious wrap
dresses, the sole decoration being the
trim and the inherent measurements. For
a designer later so identified with the
surface treatments and excitements of
apparel, Versace's first impulses were
akin to minimalism.

Sleeveless evening gown, spring–summer 1991
Partially beaded silk twill printed with polychrome images of Marilyn Monroe and James Dean
Courtesy Gianni Versace Archives

If Byzantine icons were fair game for Versace in 1991, then the icons of the 1960s were also ready for renewal and transfiguration. The movie-star idealization of Andy Warhol, more recently described as "The Warhol Look: Fashion, Style, and Glamour," was reinforced by the tandem of Monroe and Dean. By the time Versace appropriated these images, not only were both stars dead but so too was Warhol. Versace employed icons that are implicated in a lesser history than those of Byzantium but that were nonetheless historical by 1991. His interest was not in truly "contemporary" art but in Warhol as an Old Master, though the personal affinities and sensibility for media and self-projection were also subjectively keen for Versace.

Strapless evening dress, fall–winter 1989
Polychrome-beaded and embroidered
black synthetic mesh
Courtesy Gianni Versace Archives

The artists Robert and Sonia Delaunay,
and their jagged, bristly, and colorful
modern planes, were a stimulus to
Versace, especially given that Sonia
Delaunay had worked in fashion, and in
other design forms, and was one of the
first promoters of the kind of universal
artist-designer that Versace wanted to be.

Strapless dress, spring–summer 1997
White-and-black hand-painted and
appliquéd silk chiffon
Courtesy Gianni Versace Archives

The fragile, suspended world of an
Alexander Calder mobile is re-created in
the delicate scrim and layers of a Calder
dress by Versace. Versace created a
homage to the artist, but it is a knowing
one that captures the artist in a
comparable suspension rendered in a
floating modern dress.

Evening gown, fall–winter 1984–85
Black metal mesh with gold and copper
design motif
Courtesy Gianni Versace Archives

Metal mesh served Versace as the
abstract canvas, irresistible to the color
blocks and intervals that we associate
with the history of abstract painting.
Ultimately, Versace was more drawn to
the narrative forms, but his regard for
the artists Gustav Klimt, Vassily
Kandinsky, Joan Miró, and Alexander
Calder, and for modernist painting in
general testifies to an acute interest in
abstraction as well.

H·ISTORY

**Evening dress (detail), fall–winter
1997–98**
Silver-tone metal mesh with Greek-cross
appliqués
Courtesy Gianni Versace Archives

The mosaic tesserae are the common
ground of landscape, figures, and crosses
in such architectural examples as the
Romanesque churches in Ravenna, and
similarly, Versace used the metal surface
throughout a piece, equalizing the soft
drapery and the rigid form of the cross.
The complicated surface of the metal
mesh, read from afar as a shimmer, is the
logical counterpart to the mosaic, melded
from a distance but multivalent up close.

Gianni Versace was an optimist Atlas to a history that never seemed
burdensome to the designer. In Ingrid Sischy's smart summary, the one
word by which to characterize and remember Versace is fearless. Dame
History, formidable and intimidating to many creatives, never scared
Versace; he was fearless and ready to assume that history was indivisible
from contemporary design and from contemporary living. So gladly, so
gleefully did Versace cull from history that the accustomed archaeological
dust never attached itself to Versace's history. Instead, it was a splendid
combination of objective and subjective. Versace focused on four
important epochs: classicism, Byzantium, the eighteenth century, and the
1920s and 1930s (Madeleine Vionnet, Madame Grès, and Art Deco). The
history that Versace made has an antiquarianism and visually aware base
but is also a fiction as apparent as any invention of tradition. For example,
the Versace classicism, distilled in the logo of the Medusa now perhaps as
twentieth-century an image as a Nike swoosh, was not Johann
Winckelmann's but neither was that eighteenth-century art historian's
history purely objective. Rather, we know that history to be a dreaming
desire. History itself may be a muse as much as it is a chronology.

    For Versace, history was the legacy needed for contemporary
imagination. The classical draperies he perfected were not correct to art or
history. They have their debt to Cecil B. DeMille and their place in
Versace's imagination of a vigorous, sensuous, pagan world. Versace's
eternal prostitute takes her place in historical garb as a Roman slave girl

Sleeveless dress with opened bust-seam, fall–winter 1994–95
Leopard-print silk velvet and gold-tone metal mesh
Courtesy Gianni Versace Archives

A dress can be slashed, in which case its cut through to the body is an after-the-fact and additional gesture. In this instance, Versace did not slash but characteristically found his gap within the design. Leaving the gap and its corresponding drape from the bust-seam can appear accidental or incidental in a way no slash would ever be. Deconstruction as a fashion metaphor has often been a matter of destroying what is wholly made. But in the most talented hands—Rei Kawakubo for Comme des Garçons, for example—the knowledge of pattern and draping allows the design to render a select detail incomplete or unconnected. Versace's boast that he always draped is consequential when he not only constructs through draping but also deconstructs.

often with a skirt shorter than the 1920s length but looking most like the Technicolor lustiness of "epic" classical films.

Classical drapery came to Versace not with the propriety of Grès hemlines, which reach the floor in the manner of a Roman matron. Versace mixed Grès with Federico Fellini, coming up with a slave girl out of narrative art as much as out of historical evidence, but showing leg and thigh. For the Roman dresses, Versace did not reconstruct the Roman Empire; he preferred a glory in contemporary and libidinous imagination, rendering bordello Rome in its decadence and what Versace imagined as a culture in Italy of unembarrassed sexuality and of opulence similarly unblushing. Can the historian wholly confirm or deny this robust representation of history? Versace invented from a matrix of knowledge, drawing on his vast library for images out of history but insisting on extracting them from the historical disposition into a boisterous sensibility of the contemporary.

Versace's translation of Byzantium derived from his inspection of artifacts and his certainty that he could perform something akin. The mosaics of Ravenna did not hush Versace among all the international tourists; it is as if history inspired Versace to say "I can do that," even with regard to the most venerated and monumental traditions. Even the piety of monumental crosses and Virgin and Child in mosaic tesserae did not daunt Versace, who manifestly worked in a secular time and in a carnal, sensuous manner. Ravenna was an inspiration. At a later point, in 1997, The Metropolitan Museum of Art's exhibition "The Glory of Byzantium" cast Versace back into that incense-imbued world of dreams, glitter, and monumentality.

Versace's Byzantine collections called upon specific characteristics of his work. His recurrent interest in the heavy encrustation of metal embroidery corresponded to the luster of Ravenna's colorful and shining mosaics. Shrewdly, Versace rendered his Byzantium in weighty ornamentation, but he also intuited another Byzantine premise. The radiant mosaic walls of Ravenna that transmute mass into splendid message are in marked contrast to the heaviness of the construction itself. In like manner, Versace's 1997 Byzantine dresses are leather, a surface we are least likely to associate with a crust of embroidery. The result is that we have an implacable field that is made miraculous in the presence of the sparkling, story-giving surface, just as we experience on entering a Ravenna building.

For Versace, such historical references are not re-creation; they are the re-situation of the effects of history to a new circumstance in apparel. In like manner, Versace's extravagant *dix-huitième*, an amalgam of art's representation and fashion's grandiose silhouette, skims or channel-surfs the eighteenth century for the dispositions he craves: ribald sensuality worthy of Casanova's account of the court or Fielding's revelation of upwardly mobile lives; the flagrantly ornate world of horror vacui decoration, delighting in rococo excess and letting the *fêtes galantes* of the era seem even more suggestive as skirts open and bras announce love-plays and sweet elegance; and a silhouette of ballooning skirt topped not with a rib-grinding corset and bodice but with a top of deep décolletage and rib-revealing closeness to the body.

About dress inspired by the column-and-cylinder decades of the twentieth century, Versace respected both the dressmakers and the artists of the 1920s and 1930s; he understood their discovery of the flat in modern dress as a counterpart to his own modernist tendencies and his own desire to drape the dress to fall against the body. But one principle alone was not borrowed in this case. Versace loved the circles and simplified decoration of the time, suggesting that the ornate even for Versace succumbed in some way to the International Style, with its decoration that is solely determined and required by function.

History, never a burden for Versace, was treated with the legerdemain of a designer who wanted to extract the essence of the historical example when it accorded with a contemporary need. In this, we have the model of a contemporary history and of the historicism that can enlighten the creative process.

Evening dress, fall–winter 1994–95
Gold-tone metal mesh
Courtesy Gianni Versace Archives

As always, Versace offered himself challenges in dressmaking, absorbing what had begun as simple, boxlike rectangles of metal mesh into the soft drapery of a style that equivocated between the 1920s and classicism. If the wet drapery of classical sculpture could be emulated by the languorous jerseys and silks of the 1920s, then why not try to render the style in the metal mesh that Versace deftly took into a process of draping?

**Evening gown with asymmetrical hem,
spring–summer 1995**
Draped and pleated light-blue
synthetic jersey
Courtesy Gianni Versace Archives

In one of his most blatant examples,
Versace demonstrated his Fellini-like
ability to respect history and to eroticize
it and render it hyperbolic and
unforgettable. This is a strumpet of the
decadence of the Roman Empire, the
prostitute emergent from history. But
Versace's passionate history is not
without artistic evidence: as strident as
this image may be, it is based on his
equivalent to ancient statuary's wet
drapery. But surely, his is not the history
of high-school text: it is the erotic·
pageant and history expanded in terms
of our current culture and ideas.

Evening gown, fall–winter 1984–85
Gun-metal gray metal mesh studded with
rhinestones
Courtesy Gianni Versace Archives

As hard and cold as metal might be,
Versace draped it as if it were a liquid
fabric, defying all the austerity of gun-
metal gray and the heaviness of
additional rhinestones. Versace treated
the material as if it were gossamer, even
when it was not.

One-shoulder evening gown
Cream silk satin and chiffon with silver-bead embroidery
Courtesy Gianni Versace Archives

The one-shoulder-draped and manipulated gowns of Madame Grès were a great inspiration to Versace, who let a simple neoclassical line inflect the natural flow of the drapery. Even before the "Madame Grès" exhibition held in the fall of 1994 at The Costume Institute, The Metropolitan Museum of Art, on being told that the exhibition was being planned, Versace exclaimed that she had probably been the greatest inspiration to him among all designers in history.

Evening dress, fall–winter 1997–98
Silver-tone metal mesh with Greek-cross
appliqués
Courtesy Gianni Versace Archives

The mosaic tesserae are the common
ground of landscape, figures, and crosses
in such architectural examples as the
Romanesque churches in Ravenna, and
similarly, Versace used the metal surface
throughout a piece, equalizing the soft
drapery and the rigid form of the cross.
The complicated surface of the metal
mesh, read from afar as a shimmer, is the
logical counterpart to the mosaic, melded
from a distance but multivalent up close.

Evening gown, fall–winter 1997–98
Gold-tone metal mesh with Greek-cross
appliqués
Courtesy Gianni Versace Archives

The heavy metal dresses of the season,
weighing in at a shoulder-numbing
twenty pounds, are Christian soldiers of
a type that perhaps only Versace could
have envisioned. They imply the
considerable physical power of the
woman, suggesting a Xena heroine
among fashion models, but they also
convey the emotional power of the cross.
The hard surface of both dress and cross
serves as the equivalent of the mosaic
field and surface of the Byzantine crosses
of Ravenna. In her memorial recollection
of Versace, editor Ingrid Sischy
remembered the zeal of Versace when
leading her on a visit to Ravenna, a place
of great ardor for the designer.

Dress, fall–winter 1997–98
Black leather embroidered with Greek-
cross motif
Courtesy Gianni Versace Archives

In the Atelier Versace collection inspired
by The Metropolitan Museum of Art's
"The Glory of Byzantium" exhibition,
Versace returned to the great crosses he
had used in the earlier 1990s. Risking
sacrilege, Versace employed a symbol as
potent as the cross in pursuit of secular
fashion. The probability of being
criticized is often inhibiting to fashion
designers and to clothing's wearers, given
the necessary social function of the art.
But Versace could defy or at least mystify
the Church at least as much as he defied
and mystified the middle class who
would find such an incendiary gesture
offensive. In this sense, though, Versace's
design is not about being ingratiating; it
is about pursuing a vision.

Byzantine halter ensemble, fall–winter 1991–92
Polychrome beaded and embroidered black leather, black silk satin, and chiffon
Courtesy Gianni Versace Archives

Versace solicits interpretation. This ensemble requires some explanation, not only for the religious imagery but even for the presence of the leather jacket. As I argued at the time ("Sailing to Byzantium: A Fashion Odyssey, 1990–1991," *Textile & Text* 14:2, 1991): "But a Virgin and Child taken from mosaic to embroidery, gearing down the scale but keeping even the process more or less intact, is to declare representation an affinity with clothing and apparel something other than an uninterpreted, unintelligible field of design. What cannot be said about this [Versace] clothing is that it is meaningless.... Versace takes a supremely recognizable image and applies it to clothing to make explicit his demand that clothing is an eloquent, rhetorical mode." Versace knew this imagery to be provocative, and he chose to be a provocateur.

Suit, fall–winter 1991–92
Polychrome-printed silk velvet
Gift of Anne H. Bass, 1993
(1993.345.5 a–c)

Versace's romanticism and synaesthesia
are suggested in this elegant suit that
places romantic painting and dance at
the service of the fashion designer's most
tender emotions and the textile printer's
consummate mastery. Art history, always
at the designer's beck and call, mollified
Versace's sensibility in the early 1990s to
enable him to make the smart suits and
tailored daywear that emerged in the
1990s to accompany his more famous
(and infamous) eveningwear.

Bustier ensemble, spring–summer 1992
Embroidered, appliquéd, and beaded
blue silk moiré and blue denim
Courtesy Gianni Versace Archives

Modern dress in silhouette, the bustier
and jacket are in surface decoration
evocative of the eighteenth century. The
notable décolletage of eighteenth-century
separate bodices may be suggested by the
bustier, but the irony between the two
epochs appears chiefly in the modern suit
jacket offered with the decoration of the
ancien régime. It is as if Versace had all
the parts of each era but only wanted to
make a wanton jigsaw puzzle,
juxtaposing various parts and not quite
playing by the rules.

Evening ensemble, spring–summer 1992
Denim and polychrome-printed silk faille
Courtesy Gianni Versace Archives

The open gown of the eighteenth-century French court gave Versace license to offer the most extravagant version there-of. The sweet games of love that might have intrigued a court were not Versace's milieu. Instead, he made his woman more courtesan than court lady. With, however, a wonderful comprehension of eighteenth-century dress, Versace released all the potential for sensuality and love play.

Evening ensemble, spring–summer 1992
Navy-blue denim, gold-and-black
baroque-patterned silk faille
Courtesy Gianni Versace Archives

This evening outfit steps out of the
candlelight of the eighteenth century
with a stiffened skirt, petticoat-like
interventions and a palimpsest of lace,
and wondrous baroque silk with a
network of horror vacui decoration. But
never content to let a style rest in one
epoch, Versace lurched back into
twentieth-century sportswear with a
denim top. Yet even as he gave us the
bodice of a cowgirl, he also understood
eighteenth-century décolletage. While the
mannequin is seen here from the back,
we might expect the runway view with
several buttons unbuttoned: the effect of
a voyeur's Versailles rendered in rodeo
denim.

Evening ensemble, spring–summer 1988
Beaded and embroidered red net and
rose-printed red synthetic twill
Courtesy Gianni Versace Archives

A sheer bodice tops a leg-revealing skirt
of eighteenth-century style, its
unrestrained floral pattern speaking of
both Versace's excesses and those of the
eighteenth century. The skirt opens up
and falls to the sides in a bagged-up,
pouched manner of the late eighteenth
century. It is clear that this is not by any
means historical re-creation, yet it is
shrewdly aware of how high-spirited and
how profligate eighteenth-century dress
could be.

Evening ensemble, spring–summer 1992
Blue denim, gazar, and silk with gold-tone metal accessories
Courtesy Gianni Versace Archives

A vivacious print and the girlishness of a short skirt emerge from the eighteenth century but are pipelined by Versace right into the spirit of the twentieth century, more so as accompanied here by a denim jacket. Again and again, Versace evoked the eighteenth century only to confront it with more casual and more modern principles.

Asymmetrical one-shoulder evening gown, fall–winter 1997–98
Yellow rayon jersey and black leather
Courtesy Gianni Versace Archives

Indebted to Madame Grès, but rendered shockingly disruptive by the intervention of black leather, this evening gown is Versace's own version of the 1920s. In a famous photograph, probably intended chiefly for a process demonstration, a Grès mannequin exposes one breast in an asymmetrical draping. It is as if Versace took that idea and added one of his leather dresses to incorporate his version of propriety. Yet, by setting the leather as apparent contrast to the draping of the jersey, Versace made no effort to reconcile; he only disordered his examplar in Grès, making the 1920s look provocative in the 1990s.

Evening gown with asymmetrical draping and gathering, fall–winter 1997–98
Pink silk jersey
Courtesy Gianni Versace Archives

The historical source here is clearly Madame Grès, but Versace replaced the French designer's discreet elegance with his own penchant for the vampish and glamorous. Grès emphasized the classical and the comfortable. Versace displaced those characteristics with his sexy siren.

Evening gown, spring-summer 1997
Appliquéd purple silk chiffon
Courtesy Gianni Versace Archives

The ease and innate modernity of teens
and twenties dresses enthralled Versace.
Sheer layers allow dressmaking to stand
out and display print and decoration.
This classic modernism was clearly
Versace's great alternative to body-
hugging tightness and the look of the
prostitute. It assumes a lyricism for the
designer, still letting the body be
expressed but far less overtly erotic than
in other instances.

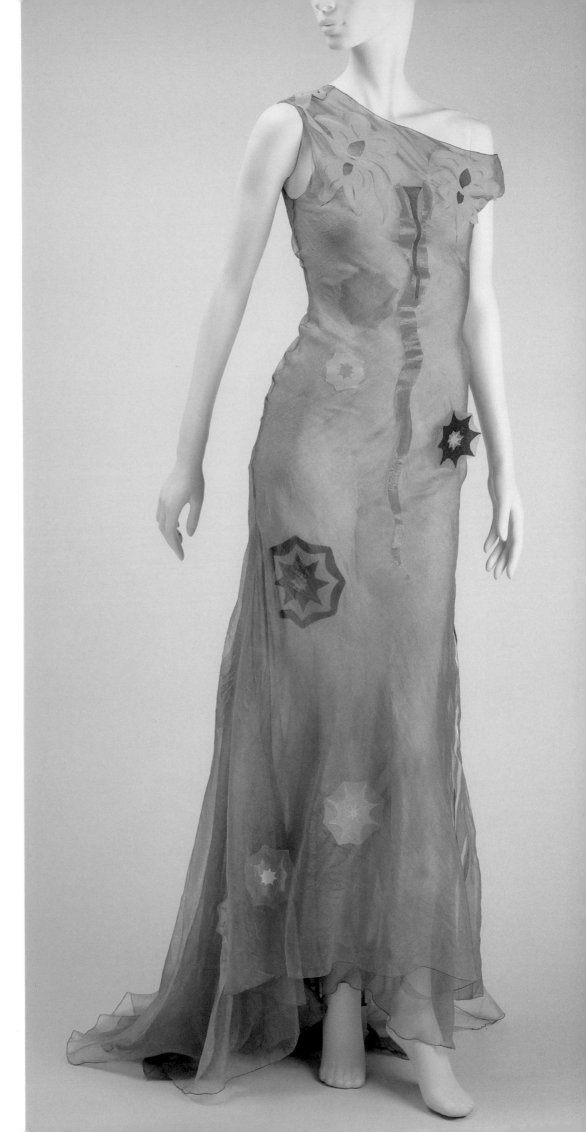

Evening dress, spring–summer 1995
Purple silk chiffon with satin appliqués
and beaded shoulder straps
Courtesy Gianni Versace Archives

The tuniclike layering of 1920s style is
suggested by Versace in this evening
dress that in silhouette might even honor
Poiret, but that is gossamer and body-
clinging in a way that shows off in the
hot light of the contemporary runway.

Evening gown, spring–summer 1997
Yellow silk chiffon with circular yellow-
and-mustard satin appliqués
Courtesy Gianni Versace Archives

Diaphanous effects encase the body in
gossamer cylinders of forms, evoking the
principles of twentieth-century fashion.
For the teens and the twenties, when
these forms originated, they suggested a
new sexuality, but Versace rendered
obvious the connection between these
floating forms and his joy of the beauty
perceived along with the gauzy surface.

**Evening dress (and detail),
spring–summer 1982**
Beaded and printed blue silk chiffon
Courtesy Gianni Versace Archives

This chiffon tube epitomizes the new
cylindrical fluidity and the cubist clarity
of the fashion new in the 1920s,
enhanced by the further referencing to
Art Deco decoration in Mediterranean
colors. It is as if Versace took his favorite
fashion designers of that period and put
them in concert with the best in
contemporaneous painting and
decorative arts.

Evening gown, spring–summer 1997
Mustard-and-orange silk chiffon
Courtesy Gianni Versace Archives

Sweetly redolent of Mycenaean
civilization, this dress of an Art Deco
archaeology also expresses the 1990s,
enhancing the body and utilizing the
contemporary disposition to sheer, body-
revealing form.

Evening gown, fall–winter 1987–88
Black metal mesh and synthetic lace
Courtesy Gianni Versace Archives

The early years of the twentieth century
rendered fashion cylindrical and with
cling that would adhere not to an
artificial structure but to the body itself,
and Versace brought the same idea to
this dress that uses the teens and twenties
style but clearly identifies the modern
woman. The presence of a train seems
historical; the cleaving to the bust and
ribs seems erotic.

Evening tank dress (detail),
spring–summer 1996
Black synthetic net with black leather
appliqués and beading
Courtesy Gianni Versace Archives

In this unusual use of leather for small
applied decoration, Versace
demonstrated his ability to equalize the
elements of his dressmaking. Leather is
not a harsh and intractable substance;
instead, it floats as a delicate touch
on net.

Gianni Versace's materials hold the surprise of Robert Rauschenberg's
plethora of media in painting and sculpture. He used traditional materials
of fashion, but pushed them toward their limits. Lace, flickering with
flirtation in Versace dresses, could be combined with leather, and leather
could even be imparted to the lace and mesh of a fabric ground. Lace
could be pleated. It was as if art school was in session and the
dressmaking academy had been dismissed, though all their techniques
were fair game. In other instances, Versace made the dressmakers—whose
very art he identified with—the ones who were challenged, bringing to
them industrial plastics, heavy leathers, and other materials more
customary for automobile upholstery than for high fashion. Versace's
favored materials are surprisingly diverse in their traits: puckered cloth
and that which will hold to the body shape as clinging smooth form;
bristly plastics laden with embroidery to supple metal meshes; leather
rendered like fabric and see-through polyvinyl chloride (industrial plastic).

The incorporation of new and vernacular materials into the art of
fashion was an inevitable outcome of Versace's mission to annul class
distinctions and to let style and fashion be more democratic. Therefore,
the tough materials and bright shine of dresses that look like they should
be cleaned not by the laundress but by a wet sponge are indicative of the
designer's desire to experiment, but paramountly to enlarge. In material, as
well as in themes and in media expansion, Versace required fashion to
claim more than its convention of materials. Black leather is no longer a

Evening dress, fall–winter 1991–92
Powder-blue silk crepe, chiffon, and lace
Gift of Gianni Versace, 1993 (1993.52.2)

Like the poet determined to represent
both innovation and conformity and
structure as well, mastering the
restraints, Versace imparted every
possible complication to the elements of
lingerie dressing. He did not merely posit
the wearing of innerwear as outerwear
but combined the techniques, providing
lace, accompanying it with quilting,
adding bracing, and pleating the lace.

**Evening dress (and detail), fall–winter
1991–92**
Pale-pink silk crêpe, chiffon and lace
Gift of Gianni Versace, 1993 (1993.52.1)

This flirtatious evening dress that is little
more than the structure of a slip is just
as rich in its couture values as it is
flamboyant in flaunting sexuality. The
dazzle of dressmaking performance was
for Versace the one possible counterpart
to the sizzle of sensuality. Lace, pleating,
and quilting all meet in the small
expanse of inches of fabric. Multiple

techniques and the investment of such
couture practice in a garment that could
from a distance pass for sleazy lingerie
are Versace tenets. After all, when
Chanel seized the little black dress in
wool jersey from the maid, she had to
give it all the couture finishes to
guarantee that it was transfigured. So,
too, Versace seized the ostensibly vulgar,
imparted a panoply of technical skills,
and left the garment changed and the
spectator overwhelmed by the merger of
complete opposites.

Animal-print ensemble, spring–summer
1992
Yellow-and-black printed silk with gold-
tone metal accessories
Courtesy Gianni Versace Archives

Never too much, never too rich, and
perhaps even never too thin—Versace
added the category of willful excess and
extravagance to fashion's ability to evoke
desire. Rich printing, varied materials,
and wild coordinations are part of the
Versace aesthetic. He preferred
decadence and immoderation to any
standard of good taste. He also invoked,
as many designers do, the spirit of Diana
Vreeland, in the whirlwind of animal
prints, flamboyance, and high style.

dusky and somewhat illicit world of motorcycle jackets but rather is
employed structurally. Moreover, leather is not a male prerogative for
Versace. Of course, other and earlier designers had used leather for
womenswear, especially Yves Saint Laurent in his pioneering work. But
Versace cast the referencing of leather back and forth between the
templates of menswear design such as motorcycle jackets and the
consummately womenswear leather he had made into skirts going back to
the 1970s. Leather is studded, but leather can also be quilted; its bits
become the geographic integers of a mesh map, or it can constitute a field
upon which the delicacy of embroidery seems even more fragile on a
staunch skin; and its practical application is mingled with its most
symbolic and most transgressive use in S & M.

Of all the materials advanced by Versace, plastic is the
quintessential and the most controversial. Transparency was an easy cause
for twelfth-century Gothic architect Abbot Suger, but it is a very difficult
one for contemporary fashion. It risks the very invisibility of the emperor's
new clothes, but it also can suggest possibilities for a modern Cinderella.
Versace honored a fashion convention in shielding the inside, where it
grazes the skin, with a soft skin, exposing relatively little of the wearer's
body to the plastic itself. The spectator's anxiety suggests that there is even
greater discomfort to the viewer than for the wearer.

Versace answered to the early-twentieth-century Italian artists'
Futurist Manifesto, when he introduced new materials to fashion and

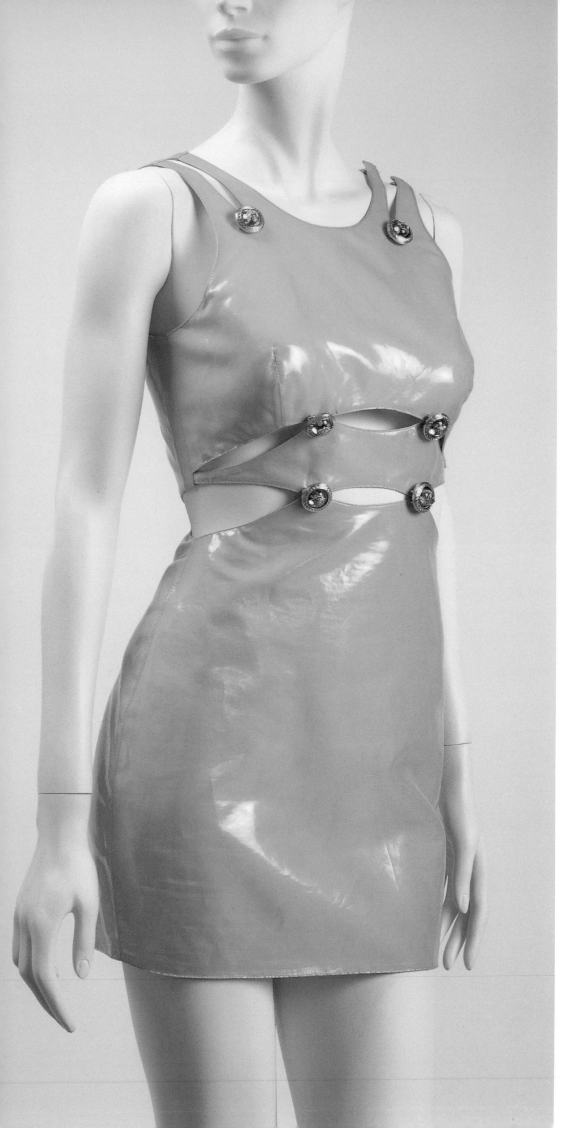

**Tank dress with cutout midriff,
fall–winter 1994–95**
Yellow vinyl
Courtesy Gianni Versace Archives

Risking reference to the 1960s but bold
enough to speak to the 1990s are
Versace's uses of the recalcitrant material
of vinyl with a dressmaker's deftness of
hand. It is perhaps difficult to imagine
such dresses as other than an Austin
Powers parody of the Sixties, but Versace
made the dress so much his signature
that we may think 1960s, but we still
remember—and are saved by the fact—
that we are in the 1990s.

**Tank dress with cutout midriff,
fall–winter 1994–95**
Fuchsia vinyl
Courtesy Gianni Versace Archives

Versace assembled a conclusive catalogue
of the horrors of the middle-class
sensibility. Brightly colored vinyl has to
be of top rank on such a list of anathemas.
Versace seized the contemptible materials
and acted as if he were dealing with silk
or wool. This is the tour de force
performance of the artist who knows
exactly what alienates his audience and
who knows equally well that he can
perform magic using the reviled
materials.

insisted on new uses for some old textiles and techniques. In trading with the vernacular, Versace was perhaps only continuing the great tradition of Chanel and others. In going beyond fashion for new resources, he may have been preceded by Elsa Schiaparelli, but his enterprising and far-reaching search for materials feels even more like an artist's endless forage for the best material, however unconventional or even unknown, through which to discover form.

Dress, fall–winter 1995–96
Cream wool with clear vinyl yoke and pockets
Courtesy Gianni Versace Archives

The use of clear vinyl causes this wool dress to seem more glued to the body, the transparency suggesting both coverage and noncoverage. In the syndrome of the emperor's new clothes, the vinyl overwhelms the more traditional material and makes the dress seem to vanish.

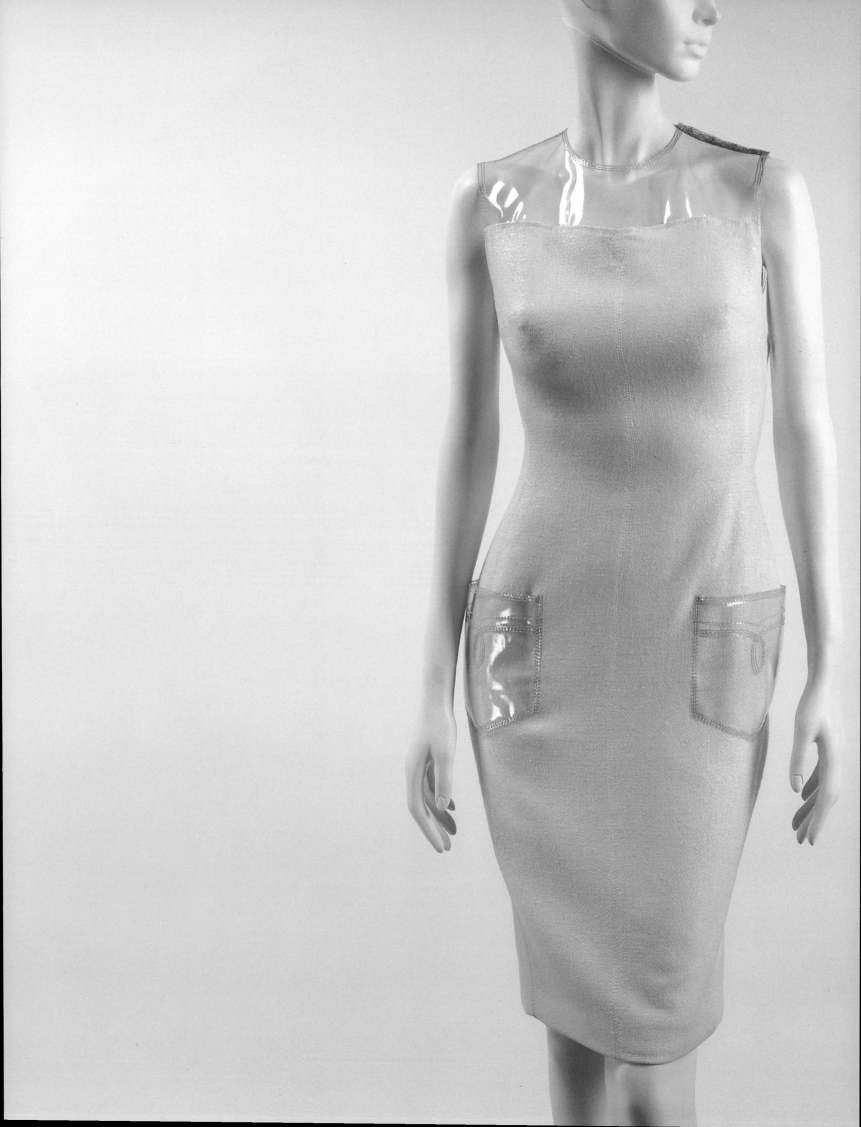

Coat, fall–winter 1992–93
Quilted black leather with fur trim
Courtesy Gianni Versace Archives

Versace's leathers have not the planes of
hard jackets but the stuff of sculpture,
and ultimately the stuff of dreams.
Concavity and convexity, reinforced by
the quilted grid, give the leather a vitality
by making the material always appear
light, almost inflatable. Even Pop
sculptures by Niki de Saint-Phalle and
Claes Oldenburg are suggested in these
alternately swelling and compressed
shapes.

Evening tank dress, spring–summer 1996
Black synthetic net with black leather
appliqués and beading
Courtesy Gianni Versace Archives

As they do in his plastic dresses,
Versace's net dresses of spring–summer
1996 offer islands of scattered beading
and appliqués to present some
reasonable coverage of the body. Black
leather floats in patches in an effect that
appears to be a wholly random and
uncontrolled order.

Evening dress, fall–winter 1996–97
Silver-tone mesh with black cotton
lace trim
Courtesy Gianni Versace Archives

Lingerie, that layer formerly unseen but
very visible in the 1990s, has been
treated by many designers by showing
the delicacies and balance between
innerwear and outerwear, public and
private. But Versace was not content
with the conundrum as it existed. Rather,
he added Joan of Arc to the fray, offering
a sheer lingerie with the silver-tone
reflections of armor or, at very least,
industrial design. The effect is to
fabricate the sheer layer as undeniably
self-sufficient. Black cotton lace trim
only furthers the sense of industrial
strength and design.

Evening dress, fall–winter 1995–96
Transparent vinyl with allover
polychrome beading
Courtesy Gianni Versace Archives

Transparent plastic is distanced from
nudity only by the scattering of beading,
conceived as a kind of aleatory allover
pattern but sufficient to deflect the eye
from a direct reading of the body within.
But Versace clearly knew that this is a
scrim and a diversion with a more
important sense of addressing the body
and making the dress as see-through
as possible.

Sarong ensemble, spring–summer 1989
Beaded black synthetic net and hand-
painted brown silk velvet
Courtesy Gianni Versace Archives

The sarong came naturally from
Versace's background and expertise in
sportswear wrapping and the global
sources implied by wraps. Like his lush
skirts in sportswear, the sarong also
contains an element of surprise. The
amplitude of the fabric is largely
concealed when it is tightly draped to
the side in the sarong manner. Now in
sumptuous material, the sarong becomes
even more extravagant.

Evening gown, fall–winter 1992–93
Cut-out and banded black wool with
top-stitched wool and leather banding
Courtesy Gianni Versace Archives

The easy and tempting allusion this
collection makes to bondage and
sadomasochistic fetish created the
expected outrage in 1992. The collection
was denounced by some, reaffirming
Versace's fashion base as the
adventuresome and avant-garde. In fact,
the collection seems to refer less to The
Mineshaft or other fetish clubs than to
the means of overlacing the body with a
minimum of structure, as spaghetti straps
and fashion exploration had always
done. The device may have had an
allusion that was sure to be incendiary
and judgmental for some, but the usage
was standard practice for advanced
twentieth-century fashion. This is not to
exculpate Versace from enjoying the
sensation his streetwise evocation
caused—in the manner of many
contemporary vanguard artists—but to
recognize that the prime cause was more
conservative than most thought. But
Versace was not trying to be politically
correct any more than he was trying to
be proper. He prized being labeled a
hedonist, for hedonism was the matrix of
his fashion sensibility.

**Wrap evening gown, spring–summer
1987**
Black metal mesh with beaded fringe
Courtesy Gianni Versace Archives

Extravagant though he may have been,
Versace admired fashion of astringency
and discipline; perhaps he could master
the discipline and then take the style to a
more ornate expression. His great loves
among the designers of the 1920s were
Madeleine Vionnet and Madame Grès,
each a fashion ascetic of a kind. But
Versace could also convey his romance
with the 1920s by his use of dynamic,
animated fringe and the sheathing flow
of popular 1920s style.

Strapless evening gown with matching
underpants, fall–winter 1995–96
Beaded yellow synthetic jersey
Courtesy Gianni Versace Archives

Braver than brave, Versace never took
refuge in the solemnity or importance of
his materials. Rather, a synthetic jersey in
scorching color would suffice and would,
of course, create a similar, if not greater,
spectacle, as a related long dress in
refined materials. Versace could, like
most designers, create evening gowns
with ease, but what he could do in such
singular fashion was to make one that
would stand out in the crowd on such
occasions as awards nights and openings.

Evening gown, spring–summer 1994
Crinkled cream silk satin and synthetic
lace with gold-tone metal safety-pin
ornaments
Courtesy Gianni Versace Archives

The wrinkled look of 1994 and 1995 is a
paradox. Versace was going mainstream
in many ways, but he was not going
bourgeois. One means of retaining his
outsider identity is the crumpled cloth,
even as it is massed into extraordinary
shapes. It is as if Versace was striving for
the shapes of Worth but insisting on
using punk pins and materials with a
disarray that would have shamed the
Charles Dickens *Great Expectations*
character Miss Havisham.

The *Vogue* logo, now stable, was in the
1920s capable of changing from month
to month in the hands of the creative
illustrators such as Georges Lepape,
Helen Dryden, and Benito who made
evocative covers, including logos,
suitable to the month. The logo could be
jewelry, skywriting, cloud formations,
Art Deco blocks, or the simulation of
medieval manuscript illumination. A
neckline that incorporates a *Vogue* logo
worn as a necklace might be reminds us
of the vintage illustrated covers of
Vogue.

Textile pattern, which provided a primary demonstration of virtuosity for
Versace, formed a part of the designer's avowed preference for luxuriance
and has remained so strong a touchstone that it translated successfully in
the early 1990s in tableware and home furnishings. Rich and wondrous
patterns came to be expected of Versace.

Versace used his expertise in prints to incorporate word and
image, permitting not only the fusion of design and printed message but
also the grander union of garment and graphic. In the Atelier Versace
collection for fall 1997, tour-de-force leather dresses with Japanese writing
and Chinese and Japanese symbols illustrate the interest that calligraphy,
most especially that which he could not read, held for Versace. In this
instance, the leather dress has come to serve as a kind of didactic
blackboard on which the messages of personal identity and international
understanding are inscribed. Gianni Versace's name appears in a vertical
column, a clumsy transliteration. Elsewhere, a mix of symbols of joy and
happiness contribute to the capacity of the dresses to speak even more
eloquently than in explicit languages. The presence of these words and
symbols is deferential. At the same time, these 1997 dresses remind us of
the early Versace jumpsuits with Japanese and other Asian symbols that
inspired Versace and came full circle into his last collection.

More than mere meaning applies as well to the several garments
Versace created using *Vogue* covers, not only the quite recent but vintage
ones as well. These garments connect fashion to media. For some, the

Halter evening gown, spring–summer 1991
Silk jersey printed with polychrome *Vogue* magazine motif
Courtesy Gianni Versace Archives

When *Vogue* celebrated its centennial with the book *On the Edge: Images of 100 Years of Vogue* (1992), writer Kennedy Fraser claimed: "In the main, *Vogue* has been a good friend to women." Surely its pages, covers, and ideas have played a role in the lives of many American women. Versace rendered a homage, using recent and historical covers of the journal, that acknowledges both a visual source in the world of women and the power of the media.

Jumpsuit, spring–summer 1991
Silk and synthetic net with allover polychrome beading in *Vogue* magazine motif
Courtesy Gianni Versace Archives

Seeking to justify the modernity and gender role of *Vogue*, Kennedy Fraser offered: "Outwardly, for most of the time, American *Vogue* seems to believe in a sort of feminine Utopia of ever healthier, more flat-bellied, and thoroughly fulfilled young professionals." Clothed in beaded journal covers, the woman who wears the jumpsuit that Versace offered as metaphor to the modern and efficient, recalls Versace's roots developing out of American sportswear and all that such sportswear implied for the effective and up-to-date woman. Versace's "advertising" is largely subservient to this effort to embody the modern woman as envisioned by magazine and designer.

Strapless evening dress, fall–winter 1997–98
Black leather embroidered with Japanese characters
Courtesy Gianni Versace Archives

For Versace, lover of sound and music, there was a purposeful glossolalia to the inchoate minglings of language. The declaration in Japanese, going back to his 1985 jumpsuit, is not one of a required, specific knowledge but rather of a sense of implied meaning. Versace understood every tourist's pleasurable moment when being so involved in a foreign place that one is intuitively certain, as in a dream, that everything being said is fully understood only to return then to the reality of incomprehension. Thus, the optimism present in the symbol is likewise the optimism of the dress: surety that we understand one another or will make every act of faith to communicate.

**Strapless evening dress, fall–winter
1997–98**
Black leather embroidered with
Japanese characters
Courtesy Gianni Versace Archives

Colorful and cheerful messages of the
symbols of greeting and joy literally
stand out against the field of leather.
They cause us to look at the leather
more carefully and to realize that this is
no sinister skin but instead a very
compliant material treated with the effect
of a textile. A flexible tube of leather on
the body is a primeval form of dress, but
in its utter simplicity it is no Wilma
Flintstone garb. Rather, its wrap may
suggest the simplification of the kimono.
It is as if Versace understood that dress
communicates even more instinctively or
basically than a learned language.

Man's leather jacket (detail),
spring–summer 1993
Black leather with silver-tone metal
beads
Courtesy Gianni Versace Archives

In menswear even more than in
womenswear, details are often prized.
Versace's leather fringe, with metal beads
working more or less as joints but
reinforcing the cowboy dandyism of the
jacket, testifies to such consequential
attention to details.

In the twentieth century, fashion design has focused on women. Many of
the greatest designers of the century never produced menswear. Men and
menswear are, however, intrinsic to Gianni Versace's thinking. He invented
the syndrome of the "pretty woman," the prostitute who becomes a
standard of beauty. He also invented, beginning his menswear collection
only a year after the womenswear, her counterpart, one as appropriate as
Ken is to Barbie. The proud strumpet, flaunting body and exercising a
politically incorrect sensuous femininity, is complemented by the "man
without tie," the gym-built poseur and sensualist, the lusty male.

As Versace's ideal for women is blatant sexuality, assuming
spectatorship, so his ideal for the male is overt sexuality, inviting
spectatorship both of the body revealed in draped shirts that reveal the
torso and of fetish-types of virile clothing, such as leather, fringe, and
studs. Significantly, Versace shirts are shaped and are never the boxy, full
cuts that have so long obscured the male body. A Versace shirt is more like
a blouse than the traditional man's shirt in materials, cut, and color.
Attention is given to the upper torso by draping so that the pectorals and
even the nipples come to constitute part of what the shirt reveals. As I
wrote in *The Advocate* (September 2, 1997) of Versace: "His menswear
was genuinely revolutionary, insisting on men as sex objects. He became
the standard-bearer of gay men's fashion because he eschewed decorum
and designed for desire."

Versace's manifesto *Men Without Ties*, often read only as a

Man's shirt, spring–summer 1991
Silk twill printed with polychrome
Warhol-inspired imagery
Courtesy Gianni Versace Archives

Because of the importance of men in
Versace's vision of fashion, he readily
transferred the motifs of womenswear
to menswear. The Andy Warhol inspired
imagery of Marilyn Monroe and James
Dean also appears on a Versace woman's
evening gown of the same collection.
Admittedly, not everyone would chose to
wear this shirt with bared torso as we
have pictured it, but the draping is, as in
all Versace's shirts, more body-clinging
and blouselike than is customary in
men's shirts. If the imagery can cross
over between men and women, the three-
dimensional form can also be similar.

scrapbook of images of beautiful men, goes further to provide a warrant
for the sensuous man. To be without a necktie is the metaphor to being
self-reliant after the industrial models for men's behaviors and for
menswear. Versace attempted to reverse the principle of "The Great Male
Renunciation" by which nineteenth-century men forsook their long-prized
embroideries, brilliant colors, dashes of lace, and luxurious materials for
the gray and dark-blue and black frock coats and suits that would be apt
for the sooty cities and dour tasks of modern industrialization and
management, leaving all that was beautiful and decorative to the sphere of
women. Versace wanted men to be just as sexy as women; he demanded
that they be physically open. In guaranteeing a positive aesthetic of
masculinity, Versace offered a perfect balance to the women he envisioned.

Man's ensemble, spring–summer 1992
Black-and-white printed silk and black-
and-white printed denim
Courtesy Gianni Versace Archives

Versace's Roman warriors, as his ideal
men might be described, inhabit a
classical civilization, even when outfitted
in denim. The black-and-white mosaics
of ancient times rise up in the patterns of
the jeans in black and white in a way
that may or may not be explicitly
recognized as ancient Rome. Versace's
uncanny ability to transport history into
the present is operative: after all, there
are standard men's black jeans, and there
are standard men's white jeans. But only
Versace put black and white together
and made them look like floor mosaics.

**Man's leather jacket,
spring–summer 1993**
Black leather with silver-tone
metal beads
Courtesy Gianni Versace Archives

In this fringed leather jacket, the devices
of the rodeo cowboy and the motorcycle
jacket are combined. The complication
of the fringing, articulated with metal
beads and balls, testifies to Versace's
disavowal of the austerity of menswear.
Rather, the Versace menswear ideal
always has a touch of the dandy,
smatterings of spectacle, and a hint of
historicism. If 1990s menswear has come
to schism between the body-aware and
the self-aware and the vestigial forms of
"The Great Male Renunciation," Versace
was clearly on the body's side and
aligned with spectacle. His menswear
has, of course, been popularly endorsed
by celebrities and especially by rock
entertainers.

**Man's black leather jacket,
spring–summer 1993**
Courtesy Gianni Versace Archives

In life as in design, the black leather
jacket served Versace as the menswear
version of the little black dress. It is not
a business suit; it incorporates sexuality,
and it engages versatility. For Versace
himself, it was a standard of his personal
wardrobe worn from day through
evening, casual to formal.

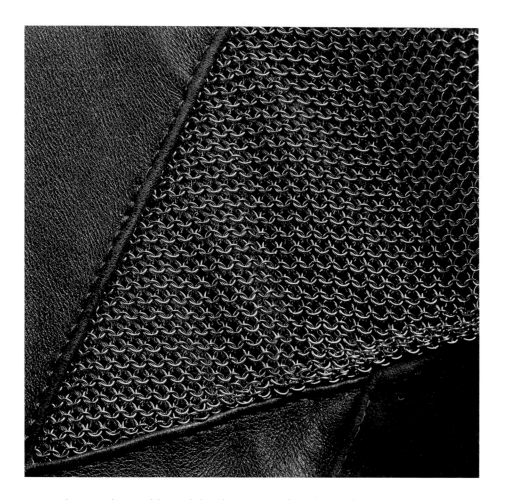

**Man's chain-mail ensemble (and detail),
fall–winter 1982–83**
Black leather with metal applied
decoration, and black denim
Courtesy Gianni Versace Archives

Of a closely related chain-mail jacket
from the same collection, I wrote in 1982:
"Perhaps we would not anticipate ... that
we would find a counterpart in apparel
design to this early post-modern
monument by Gwathmey/Siegel, but a
fall 1982 leather jacket by Gianni Versace
may suggest the same characteristics. In
the Versace jacket, the materials are most
significant not only as a sensuous surface
but also as historical allusions.... Leather
became for Versace a medieval evocation
when combined with inset steel knit
suggestive of chain mail.... As the shell of
the architecture [Whig Hall, Princeton
University] is seemingly pierced to
discover the refreshed post-modern
interior, so too the leather jacket is, as it
were, opened to reveal the inset steel
net" ("Post-Modern Menswear: Irony
and Anomaly in Men's Attire of the
1980s," *Dress*, 1982). Versace's
menswear can refer to such heroic
possibilities as knighthood and chivalry.

**Man's studded ensemble,
spring–summer 1993**
Black leather with gold- and silver-tone
metal studs
Courtesy Gianni Versace Archives

Always preferring excess, Versace offered
a proliferation of studs almost as if he
were manufacturing heavy-traction tires.
The pinpointing of a few studs would be
the customary designer translation of
popular and fetish-effect leather, even for
a Mad Max apocalyptic image, but
Versace chose to cover the body with
studs, letting the exorbitance become the
aesthetic. Virility might then reside in the
leather attire made dandified by the
lavishness of studded decoration in
contrast to its practical origin. Versace
made the leather of the streets into the
leather of luxury.

Man's Nehru-style suit,

spring–summer 1997

Gray pinstripe synthetic twill

Courtesy Gianni Versace Archives

Perverse and clever, Versace yielded to
pinstripes but not to the boardroom.
Even as his womenswear would not yield
to middle-class convention, so too
Versace resisted middle-management
menswear. Pinstripes seem almost the
contradiction of the Nehru style; the
former is a forward gesture, while
the other is a conservative convention.

**Man's jeans (and pocket detail),
fall–winter 1990–91**
Printed cotton-and-nylon blend twill
Gift of Brooks Adams and Lisa
Liebmann, 1996 (1996.237.7)

Bold Asian prints suffused even Versace
jeans in the early 1990s, as he looked yet
again to the Far East and Near East.

Even jeans were subject to Versace's
unremitting sense of decoration and his
horror vacui penchant for narrative
adornment, more or less transferring the
crowded pages of Eastern illustration to
the form of contemporary jeans. His rich
illustration is not entirely meant for
conventional reading, given that it
reverses with the pocket details.

THE DREAM

Panniered theater dress (detail), 1991
Quilted blue silk satin with black-and-
white satin appliqués
Courtesy Gianni Versace Archives

In this costume for a production of
Strauss's *Capriccio* at the Royal Opera
House in London, the fullness of an
eighteenth-century dress with petticoats
and panniers explodes into full lateral
expansion in a contemporary caricature
of the wide, extravagant dimensions.
Insinuations of modern design cover the
surface, giving the effect of abstract
pattern discernible on an eighteenth-
century silhouette.

"All the world's a stage." No one believed or lived this aphorism from
Shakespeare more fully than Gianni Versace. Creating costume for daily
life and for special occasions is the métier Versace knew well. But his
version of daily life is so spectacular, as if planned for the proscenium
rather than the street, that there is little difference between the theater
designer that he became for opera and dance and his sensibility for the
operetta of our lives.

Versace always created to the grand scale. Even the early
sportswear achievements added rich accents and set the scale bigger,
allowing blouses with deep troughs of materials above capacious skirts,
ready for the opera star to step into. By the mid-1980s, his work assumed
even more the principle of visible concupiscence, taking on the stagelike
presence of the prostitute, who was taking on the role of the diva long
established.

This selection for the dream incorporates several dresses from the
fashion repertoire that suggest the essential silhouette and the semaphore
for elegance that could transport us into the dream. Versace's little black
dress with covered-up front and uncovered back is in this category. A
woman entering a room in such a dress would suggest reserve and utmost
propriety. Even as Versace achieved mainstream status in the 1990s, a
dress this aloof, chaste, and formal would seem most uncharacteristic. But
the dress has yet to reveal itself. When seen from the back, this woman of
decorum now becomes a seductress, making a spectacular, perhaps vulgar

**Sleeveless evening dress with panniers
and oversized stole, spring–summer 1988**
Black-and-white filigree-printed silk
Courtesy Gianni Versace Archives

This evening dress with panniers
inevitably recalls the eighteenth century,
even though it is brusquely short.
Versace had made note of the Lacroix
pouf of 1987, and he created his own
version, perhaps even more graphic and
even more flirtatious in its streamlined
form. Even with a reference to another
designer of embellished and historicist
form, Versace made his own version
more addressed to the body.

exit. This is dressmaking and stagecraft for Versace. While he has canted
the fabric in order to provide the minimal juncture at the back, this dress
is theater for Versace, implying that fashion plays a dramatic role.

Versace's gargantuan ambitions for fashion included a role for it in
all the arts. To imagine the runway, the rock-and-roll concert, the opera
stage, the grand public event, and even Hollywood as a continuous
platform is what Versace did. Timeless metaphor and the eternal yearning
for synaesthesia were for the first time not in the hands of a poet,
playwright, composer, or even impresario. Chanel, Dior, Schiaparelli, and
others designed for theater and film from the experimental to the
commercial. But Versace's model for the dream, the accustomed fantasy of
fashion now endowed with a new trait of media, was that the fashion
designer was a fundamental dreamer, one who planned and not merely
one who followed other artists. Rather, this crucible for the arts was
imagined by a fashion designer.

The concept is as simple as it is startling. Creating a utopian
design or conceiving the medium of spectacle can be a fashion designer's
initiative. The fashion designer is no longer ex post facto staff to artists of
enterprise in other media. Versace dreamed a dream of the spectacle that
begins with fashion and engages every sense and every vision.

Evening slip gown, fall–winter 1996–97
Fuchsia cotton lace studded with
rhinestones
Courtesy Gianni Versace Archives

Versace understood fashion as spectacle,
allowing for "entrance dresses" that
would have knocked Edith Wharton and
all cultures of confidence. Versace's
eclectic historical range was always
expressed with the assurance of someone
who made fuchsia a great declaration
and who combined the boldness of color
with the clinging silhouette and low
neckline of the woman who wants to
shock. In another time, such a woman
might have stood for a John Singer
Sargent portrait; she might have been
Mrs. Rita Lydig, for example. Style
history has always depended upon those
women and their determined style that
was dazzling in its complete lack of
reticence. Thus, Versace created a dress
not for spectacle or theater per se, but
that is inherently the memorable "drop-
dead" dress that can bear no apology
but otherwise bares much.

Back-drape evening gown, fall–winter 1990–91
Black silk jersey
Courtesy Gianni Versace Archives

This dress, ready to surprise the viewer coming and going, symbolizes Versace's emancipation from any bourgeois values. From the front, it pleases and appeases: it is conservative social garment. From the back, the dress is pure spectacle, edging away from polite society. It is a piece of theater in itself. Of course, Versace may have been thinking about such designers as Augustabernard and Madeleine Vionnet, who in the 1920s and 1930s provided deep descent in the back, often accompanied by a high neckline in front. But Versace clearly added an *épater la bourgeoisie* twist via the extreme descent at the back.

Theater dress, 1987
Cream and black silk with three-
dimensional black chiffon sleeve caps
Courtesy Gianni Versace Archives

This dress for Herodias in a La Scala
production of Wilde-Strauss's *Salomé* is a
captivating creation for theater. Versace
thought in terms of the body-clinging
form he most admired, but he extended
the shoulders as elsewhere he extended
the hips with eighteenth-century
panniers. There, the elaboration was true
to history. Here, he did more than
Adrian or Edith Head (whom he
admired for their movie work) to make
powerful shoulders through their
extension into rectangles.

Theater dress, 1989
White silk satin appliquéd with black
silk satin, net, crêpe, and braid
Courtesy Gianni Versace Archives

This behemoth eighteenth-century dress
for Clairon in the San Francisco Opera
production of Richard Strauss's
Capriccio could sweep an entire stage,
but all of Versace's dreams of the
eighteenth century are about great
inflated dresses, triumphant music, and
male and female elegance of a kind
unequaled today. The pretext was
Strauss, but the vision is pure Versace.

Theater ensemble, 1987
Hand-painted and appliquéd silk
Courtesy Gianni Versace Archives

The features of regional dress, with its
hand-painting and sense of layering and
pastiche, are not, after all, far removed
from Versace's own characteristics of
emphatic, rich dressing. This ensemble
conveys a grandiose effect without class
pretension, projecting the full joie de
vivre of common folk and natural
exuberance. Appreciating such virtues,
Versace made a dress of extravagant,
but not necessarily costly, effects.

Panniered theater dress, 1991
Quilted blue silk satin with black-and-
white satin appliqués
Courtesy Gianni Versace Archives

In this costume for a production of
Strauss's *Capriccio* at the Royal Opera
House in London, the fullness of an
eighteenth-century dress with petticoats
and panniers explodes into full lateral
expansion in a contemporary caricature
of the wide, extravagant dimensions.
Insinuations of modern design cover the
surface, giving the effect of abstract
pattern discernible on an eighteenth-
century silhouette.

which are illustrated with striking elegance and simplicity. The section titled "The Landmarks" is a retrospective look at Versace's major achievements. "Art" sketches in Versace's relationship with various artists, such as Alexander Calder and Robert and Sonia Delaunay, and emphasizes his particular sympathy for the work of Andy Warhol. In "History," we learn about Versace's creative interpretations of the past, from Byzantine art to the classicism of Madame Grès. "Materials" demonstrates Versace's extremely unusual incorporations of industrial plastics and leather, for example, which he so successfully translated into his own personal forms. Among the costumes in "Word and Image," we find a sparkling *Vogue*-inspired gown and small black leather dresses emblazoned with Japanese characters. The section on Versace's "Men" demonstrates his revolutionary views of the sensuous male in black leather with studs and fringes, or in brilliantly patterned shirt or jean. And lastly there is "The Dream," an evocation of Versace's visions of costumes for the opera and the dance, all of which are pure theater in the hands of this designer.

In his Introduction to this volume, Richard Martin expresses the spirit of the Metropolitan Museum's tribute to Gianni Versace: "On seeing his work in a museum exhibition or in this book, it becomes clear that Gianni Versace is no mere figure of sentiment or cultural inquiry, or subject-object of the media spectacle. Under the dissecting light of a museum's examination, Versace achieves another and equally positive effect. The encyclopedic knowledge, the virtuoso performance of techniques, the sensibility to experiment, and the equilibrium between history and contemporaneity are perhaps seen even more clearly here."

192 pages; 107 illustrations, all in color; selected bibliography

The Metropolitan Museum of Art, New York

Distributed by Harry N. Abrams, Inc., New York